Avengers Assemble!

The Marvel Cinematic Universe is in disarray.

Marvel Studios' *Avengers: Endgame* follows on from the cataclysmic events of Marvel Studios' *Avengers: Infinity War*, where a divided team of Earth's Mightiest Heroes tried to fight alongside The Guardians of the Galaxy, the Masters of the Mystic Arts, Peter Parker/Spider-Man, Bucky Barnes/Winter Soldier, Okoye, and T'Challa/Black Panther, in an attempt to stave off the cosmic despot Thanos... and failed.

Now, seeking redemption from their defeat and aiming to avenge their fallen comrades, those surviving heroes who've been left behind must set aside their differences, forge new alliances, and remember how to work together as they struggle to hunt down Thanos and defeat him once and for all in what will be the ultimate conclusion to 22 films, over 10 years in the making.

THE OFFICIAL MARVEL MOVIE SPECIALS
Captain Marvel
Ant-Man and The Wasp
Avengers: Infinity War
Black Panther: The Official Movie Companion
Black Panther
Thor: Ragnarok
Marvel Studios: The First 10 Years

Spider-Man: Far From Home (July)

TITAN EDITORIAL

Editor Jonathan Wilkins
Managing Editor Martin Eden
Associate Editors Tolly Maggs
& Jake Devine
Art Director Oz Browne
Senior Production Controller Jackie Flook
Production Controller Peter James
Sales and Circulation Manager Steve Tothill

Advertising Assistant Bella Hoy
Commercial Manager Michelle Fairlamb
Senior Brand Manager Chris Thompson
Senior Publicist Will O'Mullane
Publishing Director Darryl Tothill
Operations Director Leigh Baulch
Executive Director Vivian Cheung
Publisher Nick Landau

DISTRIBUTION
U.S. Newsstand: Total Publisher Services, Inc.
John Dziewiatkowski, 630-851-7683
U.S. Newsstand Distribution: Curtis Circulation
Company
U.S. Bookstore Distribution: The News Group
U.S. Direct Sales: Diamond Comic Distributors
For more info on advertising contact
adinfo@titanemail.com

Marvel Studios' *Avengers: Endgame* published April 2019 by
Titan Magazines, a division of Titan Publishing Group
Limited, 144 Southwark Street, London SE1 0UP.
For sale in the U.S. and Canada.

ISBN: 9781787730137

Printed in the U.S.

Contributor Nick Jones
Thank you to Shiho Tilley, Christopher Troise, and
Eugene Paraszczuk at Disney for all their help.

Titan Authorized User. No part of this publication may be
reproduced, stored in a retrival system, or transmitted,
in any form or by any means, without the prior written
permission of the publisher. A CIP catalogue record for
this title is available from the British Library.
10 9 8 7 6 5 4 3 2 1

CONTENTS

THE GAME PLAN

For over a decade, across 22 movies, Marvel Studios President Kevin Feige has masterminded the Marvel Cinematic Universe, building the most ambitious film series ever conceived. As his grand plan reaches its incredible climax, Feige casts his eye over the MCU to date, and examines what it all means for Marvel Studios' *Avengers: Endgame*

Marvel Studios' *Ant-Man and The Wasp*

MARVEL STUDIOS PRESIDENT

Looking back on the more recent Marvel Cinematic Universe movies, why do you think fans connected to *Black Panther* so much?
Kevin Feige: The whole world-creation of Wakanda was paramount for [director] Ryan Coogler when he started. He wanted to stay true to some of what appeared in the comic books, but he also took a trip to Africa soon after he signed on board. He brought back with him all sorts of knowledge about the different cultures over there – ideas for color schemes, for materials, for fabrics – to infuse Wakanda with the heightened element of its comic book counterpart, but also with real, true African cultures.

He sat down with our costume designer, Ruth Carter, and our Marvel Studios visual development department led by Ryan Meinerding, and together the three of them created what I think are the best costumes we've ever had in a Marvel Studios film. You see in them the power of the Dora Milaje warriors. You see in them the border tribe, those beautiful blankets that came right out of South Africa.

What you have is these iconic characters, and these iconic looks for all the costumes. The Panther costume itself, designed by Shuri in one of my favorite scenes in the movie, is an entirely new way of making a Super Hero costume – both in the movie and behind the scenes – that is tactile, that is laced with Vibranium within the storytelling. What I love about it is Panther himself is a very dark outfit, which allows him to sneak around in the shadows, but most of the rest of the costumes are bright and bold and pretty awesome.

One of the breakout stars of *Black Panther* was Shuri, as played by Letitia Wright. What do you think made her such a hit with the fans?
Shuri is T'Challa's sister. She also happens to be one of the smartest people in Wakanda. She's the head of the Wakandan Design Group. As we were developing the movie, we always referred to her as Black Panther's Q. She is the designer who comes up with the suit, the new helmets, the weapons. Before each mission, T'Challa will go see her and basically get a rundown of the latest equipment. You not only have this fun brother-sister dynamic, but you also have this amazing, youthful, intelligent, strong woman who's in charge of the science and the engineering in Wakanda.

Letitia Wright is incredible and really brought to that character everything we hoped. Ryan Coogler saw it, and Chadwick Boseman saw it in the very first screen test that Letitia did for the movie: this strength, but also this humor. You have that brother-sister banter, which I love and which is so funny. She gives him a hard time about his footwear, but at the same time, she's designing the most amazing stuff for him. Then when the time calls for it, she puts on her own battle outfit and runs into the fray with her amazing Panther gauntlets, which was a Ryan Coogler-designed special right from the start.

So, Shuri is a little bit Tony Stark, a little bit Black Panther, but entirely herself. Seeing kids around the country being inspired by Shuri and putting on that costume and going out – not just for a costume party for Halloween, but to feel empowered – is the reason we made that movie.

Turning to *Avengers: Infinity War* and *Endgame*, would it be fair to say you took a big chance with these films, in particular the way the two movies work together?
With every Marvel Studios movie we make, we're looking to do something unique and special. With this story, we knew we were starting with *The Infinity Gauntlet* comic book series by Jim Starlin [with George Pérez and Ron Lim]. It is a classic Marvel comic book. It is an amazing, ambitious, and bold story, and we wanted to do justice to that. That story doesn't pull any punches in terms of what happens to the characters and the world, and in terms of the powers that Thanos is able to manifest once he has all the Infinity Stones and the gauntlet. So, we didn't want to slight that; we didn't want to pull any punches there either.

02

01 Kevin Feige and *Ant-Man and The Wasp* director Peyton Reed

02 Kevin Feige (center) on the set of Marvel Studios' *Thor: Ragnarok* with director Taika Waititi (left)

> ## "With every movie we make, we're looking to do something different, unique, and special."

One of the big things that happens in that comic book is the elimination of half the life in the universe, so we knew that was going to be a part of the movie. It was during early discussions with Joe and Anthony [Russo] and Chris [Markus] and Steve [McFeely], our screenwriters, that we started realizing that's how you end the first movie. Not necessarily as a cliffhanger, because we actually don't look at this as part one and part two. A lot of people understandably do, because that's how they feel walking out of the theaters: what happens next? But we looked at it as a definitive ending – just not the ending you were expecting.

Were you at all worried about how audiences would react to that decision?
One thing we've done on the 18 movies leading up to *Infinity War* within the Marvel Cinematic Universe is we screen test all of our movies. It's a great tool, a great resource, a great way to refine the storytelling of whatever film you're working on. You learn what jokes are working; you learn what thematics are working; you learn what plot twists are working, or what storytelling is confusing, or what needs to be streamlined. All of that is very helpful.

After a screening, people get a double-sided card, and they fill out answers to questions. Part of it is a little ▶

▶ section where you can just check things off: "It moves just right"; "It's too long"; "It was too slow"; "It was too fast"; "It was too predictable"; "It was too scary, too exciting." Usually the boxes that get checked are what we want. If we're working on something that we want to be humorous, people write, "Yes, it was funny." If we work on something that we want to be breathless action, people write, "We like the action." But almost every movie, they write, "Too predictable." They check that little "too predictable" box.

For a long time, I thought, "What's too predictable?" We had a big twist in this movie, a big surprise in that movie, and people would write, "I love that surprise," or, "I loved that twist," or, "I didn't see that coming." So why did you check "too predictable"? It only took me about a dozen movies or so, but I finally started to realize, "Oh, they mean the good guy wins. That's what they mean." They mean, it's a Super Hero movie – the good guy is going to win. How you get there is what

is entertaining about the movie, which they enjoyed. But they would check that little "too predictable" box because the good guy wins.

We knew what was coming with *Infinity War*, and I remember thinking, "Let's see what happens when that doesn't occur – when the heroes do not win, when you have to leave the theater of a movie where you take it for granted that the hero is going to win, and it doesn't happen." That was one of the things we were most excited about. It was risky, but we look at risks as fuel for doing the right thing. You have to be able to be scared. You have to think that you're taking a risk to get excited enough, to justify embarking on a venture as large as a Marvel Studios movie.

How confident were you in taking that risk?
We were very confident as we were working on the storyline, as Chris and Steve were writing the script, as Joe and Anth were directing the movie, as Jeff Ford

"The intention from the start, many years ago when we embarked on this two-picture journey to tie up the Marvel Cinematic Universe, was that it would be very hard to predict where *Avengers: Endgame* goes and how it gets there."

03 Rocket, last survivor of the Guardians of the Galaxy

world with their stomach dropping and tears beginning to well in their eyes, because these fictional characters have affected them. To me, that's been the pinnacle of this entire experience so far. The other side of that is we now have to deliver with *Avengers: Endgame*.

There are extraordinary stories of how people were affected by *Infinity War*...
You're right. I've heard stories. There were tears. Somebody told me a story at the premiere that they brought a guest, and the guest was crying at the end of the movie. This person said, "We're at a big premiere, oh, geez, they're embarrassing me." Then they looked around, and everybody was crying. At the same time, I think there's a sense when you get emotionally involved – and I know as a film fan myself – that you appreciate the fact that you've been sucked in, that you've been brought into this storyline.

I've also heard stories that people had to show their kids – or even their friends who were very upset about the ending of our movie – that, "No, look, they've already announced another movie. Look at the release schedule: there's another movie in May," and that people would go, "Really?" and figure it out.

What's exciting for us as we now embark on *Avengers: Endgame* is that nobody has guessed what's going to happen. The intention from the start, many years ago when we embarked on this two-picture journey to tie up the Marvel Cinematic Universe, was that it would be very hard to predict where *Avengers: Endgame* goes and how it gets there.

After the devastating end of *Infinity War*, how do the heroes find their resolve to continue in *Endgame*?
All of the remaining heroes deal with the events of the end of *Infinity War* differently. All of them are used to trauma of one kind or another. None of them are used to being defeated so thoroughly by a single antagonist. They are trying to figure out how that happened, and why that happened.

Tony Stark has been worried about a cataclysmic event since the first *Avengers* film. He was suffering through PTSD in *Iron Man 3*. He talked about putting a suit of armor around the world in *Age of Ultron*, which ▶

was cutting the movie together, that this was our ending. It wasn't until the final week or so before release that I started to get scared, that I started to think, "Oh, what are people going to do?" Because we'd screened the movie, and even after a friends and family screening, or anytime people get to see a free movie, they usually clap at the end. There was no clapping at the end of an *Infinity War* screening. People liked the movie, but they were just stunned.

We were heading into the premiere, and I was like, "Well, let's see." It ended up being exactly the reaction that we wanted, because people were shocked. People were holding back tears. As painful as that might be in the moment of the end of a movie experience, it actually means people have connected to these characters. People have connected to this universe. Celebrating our 10th anniversary of Marvel Studios, there is no better indication of how far we've come, and how far the global audiences have come with us. Yes, the total gross of the movie and the box office receipts are amazing; but it's that reaction – people sitting in theaters around the

▶ unfortunately is what led him down a path to the creation of Ultron. But he always knew. Tony Stark is a futurist: he prepares for the future; he sees what other people don't. He saw something terrible happening, and he couldn't do anything about it. That is a blow to him.

But one of the great things about the Avengers – one of the great things about Steve Rogers in particular – is that no matter how hard you knock them down, they always get back up.

What was behind the decision to raise the stakes?
We wanted to do a great finale that not only had the spectacle worthy of what they were left with at the end of *Infinity War*, but with sequences and scenes and character interactions that could only be done with a crew of people that have been working together as

long as we have, and with a group of actors who have been portraying and embodying these characters as long as our actors have. So, we talk a lot about the culmination of 22 movies leading up to *Avengers: Endgame*.

Why do you think Thanos has been such a hit?
The answer to why Thanos worked is Josh Brolin. The reason Thanos is now this iconic movie villain is because they understand where he was coming from is because of Josh Brolin. People put "villain" in quotes when they're talking about Thanos.

We introduced Thanos for the first time at the end of the very first *Avengers* film. Joss Whedon wrote in the very end of his draft this little tag where a character turns around and smiles. We didn't say the name, but fans recognized that purple profile. That was the beginning of planting a

> "One of the great things about the Avengers is that no matter how hard you knock them down, they always get back up."

04 Feige and Robert Downey Jr. share a moment on the set of the film that started it all, Marvel Studios' *Iron Man*

It was an idea that came about pretty late in development, and I decided we needed an actor. It was a very small scene, wouldn't require much time for an actor, but we needed somebody quickly. I thought that face and that presence of Josh Brolin would be incredible, not just for the little bit we wanted in *Guardians*, but should we ever proceed into the future, you want an amazing actor. But there wasn't much time, and we required a simple yes. Often times there's a lot of negotiating, a lot of convincing. Josh said yes right away.

I don't think he even understood quite what he was in for at that time, because he came to us soon afterwards saying, "You know, a lot of people know Thanos. I've done a lot of movies in my career, but never have people been so interested about something I haven't done yet," after it had been announced or it had leaked that he was playing the part of Thanos.

What do you think Josh Brolin has brought to the character of Thanos in *Infinity War* and *Endgame*?
Even with the little bit in *Avengers*, the little bit in *Guardians*, the little bit in *Avengers: Age of Ultron*, we always knew that we would have to deliver big in *Infinity War*. If you're going to tease something out for years and years, you better deliver once you get there.

Right from the start in that opening scene in *Infinity War*, Josh came to deliver. It's really remarkable what he's done with that character, and the way he's done it. Yes, the technical achievements are impressive – the work that Dan DeLeeuw and his team have done in visual effects is unprecedented and amazing – but it all goes back to the performance that Josh did, not just on the set but also in a motion capture environment. He nails the performance every single time, whether he's on a real set with real actors, or whether he's on a motion capture volume with technicians surrounding him. He goes into a place, which is what great actors do, and he delivers an amazing performance. I think people recognize that now. I'm glad that now the technology is such that you see that performance with every little, minute bit of motion within his eyes and within his face.

Thank goodness he did and that Thanos lived up to the anticipation, and the tease was worth it. He spent a lot of time sitting in chairs before *Infinity War*, so we knew the minute he stood up, he had to get to work. ▶

Marvel Studios' *Iron Man*

flag saying, "We could be going *here*; we could be building towards Thanos." People who read the comic books knew that meant building towards *The Infinity Gauntlet*.

But even after the first *Avengers*, people thought, "That's too ambitious, you can't do *The Infinity Gauntlet* as a movie." We weren't sure about it either at that point. We were just working on Phase Two, and one of the biggest films of Phase Two was *Guardians of the Galaxy*. We were intentionally bringing in new characters, setting the stage again, and going to a place where even many hardcore comic book fans had no knowledge about these characters. Within that, we found an opportunity late in the process to include Thanos. The character of Gamora and the character of Nebula were tied in to the comic history of Thanos, so it seemed appropriate to add him there.

> "Something I love is hearing people going to see *Infinity War*, loving it, and then going back and watching all the movies again in a single run."

▶ **With his ultimate goal now achieved, where do we pick up with Thanos in *Endgame*?**

That's the question, isn't it? Thanos has achieved what he wanted to achieve. We saw him at the end of *Infinity War*. One of the reasons why we don't consider *Infinity War* a cliffhanger is because the end of the movie is not the heroes disappearing, the heroes dying, the heroes turning to dust. The end of the movie is Thanos, content – a little worse for wear, on a planet in a rather shockingly idyllic environment, doing exactly what he told us he would do: sitting and looking upon a grateful universe. He succeeded, and that's the end of the film. Will the Avengers try to stop him? Maybe. They'll try. But they didn't have much luck before, and I don't think he's worried that they'll have much luck now. So, Thanos is very content, very pleased. I think he knew it cost him everything. We saw him with little Gamora right after he snapped that gauntlet, and she asked what it cost, and he said everything. So, I don't know that he's a happy guy, but I think he's a content guy that he had achieved what he set out to.

What can you say about the importance of Captain Marvel to *Endgame*?

At the very end of *Infinity War*, after the credits, we find the tag with Maria Hill and Nick Fury. They're in a city where Thanos' snap has occurred. It's one of the largest-scale versions of people disappearing we see in the movie – cars crashing, a helicopter crashes into a building – and Nick Fury does something he's never done before: he looks scared. He looks very nervous when Maria Hill disappears in front of him.

He makes a beeline to his bag, and in that bag is something he's been carrying with him for many, many years. He hits a button, and we see it drop to the ground: it's an old pager from the '90s, and it's beeping and it's beeping. Then people who know the Cinematic Universe and know the comics recognize it as Captain Marvel's logo.

How did he get that? What does that mean? Of course, that's what the *Captain Marvel* movie is about. And if people have seen the teaser trailer, we see a pager in there, which looks very familiar. It's not modified yet, but we see it in that teaser. We learn in the *Captain Marvel* film not just about Carol Danvers and this amazing, powerful woman's journey and story, and how she got to be the most powerful character in the

Cinematic Universe, but we also learn how Nick Fury is first exposed to the intergalactic and to the super-powered characters.

It really was fun, just before we have our final conclusion, to go back, earlier than any of our other movies except for *Captain America: The First Avenger*, and introduce the beginning of the Avengers Initiative, and what Captain Marvel is able to bring…

What do you hope audiences take from *Endgame*?

With *Avengers: Endgame*, there are 22 movies now. We, of course, have seen them all – we've made them all, and we've been a big part of it. But something I love is hearing people going to see *Infinity War*, loving it, and then going back and watching all the movies again in a single run, which I think is just great.

I love the idea that people are revisiting them again, certainly in the buildup to *Endgame*. We want people to feel, hopefully, very touched and moved at the story that we tell, but also want to go back and explore it again. Yes, to be excited for what's to come in the new adventures and the new saga to come, but to look back on the entirety of what we will now call the Infinity Saga, from the first *Iron Man* movie to *Avengers: Endgame*, and watch it again.

How does it feel to have finally arrived at this point?

It's been a journey for Marvel Studios, and it's been a journey for 10-plus years for our fans, for people who enjoy going to the movies. The reaction to the end of *Infinity War*, when half their favorite characters dissipated and turned to dust, really was indicative of how emotionally connected the world has gotten to these characters. It is triply so for those of us working day in, day out on these movies – and certainly the actors who have been portraying these characters for many years – because there's been the personal journey for all of us involved in these movies. We reflect back on where we were 12 years ago, auditioning actors for Tony Stark and having hopes and dreams of where this could go with Marvel Studios.

But also, for the people watching the movies, they know these characters now, in some ways better than we do. I always believe once we finish a movie, it goes out to the world and it belongs to the world. It's not ours. It's ours up until that point, but then just like movies that I loved as a kid that I consider mine more than the filmmakers', once you release it into the world, it belongs to the world.

So, there are moments that will reward people who've been following along, casually or in depth, in ways that are emotional and in ways that I don't think you find very often in movies. Sometimes there are great novel series that go on for many years, where you grow with the characters. Sometimes there are television series that go on for many years, where you can grow and change as the characters grow and change. But in movies that doesn't happen so much, and it's really humbling and an honor to be a part of that. Ⓐ

05 Having recently debuted in her own movie, Captain Marvel plays a key role in Marvel Studios' *Avengers: Endgame*

THE SURVIVORS

The sudden brutality of Thanos' universe-wide attack left the Avengers in disarray with only a small number of defeated and dejected survivors left to ponder their next move.
Those still standing include...

IRON MAN

CAPTAIN AMERICA

THOR

HULK

BLACK WIDOW

HAWKEYE

WAR MACHINE

ROCKET

ANT-MAN

NEBULA

CAPTAIN MARVEL

IRON MAN

Stranded on an alien planet with Nebula, defeated by Thanos after watching Spider-Man die – Tony Stark returns in Marvel Studios' *Avengers: Endgame*. Robert Downey Jr. looks back on the Avenger that started it all.

What was your reaction to *Avengers: Infinity War*?
Robert Downey Jr.: The last eight minutes of that movie are maybe the best eight minutes in the entire history of the whole run of the Marvel Studios movies, because everyone's involved. So I was delighted.

Where do we find Tony Stark in the opening moments of *Avengers: Endgame*?
At the beginning, lest we forget those that didn't blip out of existence, we're still on Titan. So, it's all about can Tony get home and how? I think if the last real trauma we were showing in *Iron Man 3* came from when the portal opened in *The Avengers*, then I feel like the next real gut punch that Mr Stark receives is this. A lot of it is not wanting to run the risk of trying to change anything that's happened because he was one of the lucky ones who made it out, but also feeling that sense of obligation to see if he can do what he can.

How does his foresight of this weigh on him?
With Tony being an irresponsible 40-something-year-old back in the day, and now having something slightly more professorial about him, he's recognizing that he actually should have his eyes on the long game here. So there's a different set of principles that he's operating by than he had before. A lot of that has been the burgeoning effect of all of these other Avengers, and seeing how much they've put on the line.

How hard does Peter Parker's death weigh on Tony?
As a recovering sociopath, Tony's not all that touchy feely. But we know that he's pretty crazy about this kid and also really appreciates the crucible that Peter went through which we saw in *Spider-Man: Homecoming* and then obviously the continuation of that in *Avengers: Infinity War*. There is a sense that if somebody believes you're a mentor figure to them, that can be good for you because it can make you strive to be a better person.

Was it fun to pay off so many storylines?
Marvel Studios are the very best at this, and you've seen it happening in other movies that we've been enjoying since, where you can go back and you basically pillage the back catalogue. 'What are our options? What is the wish list?' Which reminds me of the first time we were at Comic Con. We were getting feedback from the fans saying, 'This is what you did, this is the kind of tone we think would be fun, we haven't seen anything like ▶

> "[Tony] is recognizing that he actually should have his eyes on the long game here."

01 Tony Stark: stranded after the events of Marvel Studios' *Avengers: Infinity War*

02 Iron Man's latest suit

02

03 Tony leaves a message for Pepper Potts

this...' Having made such inroads with all these Marvel franchises, you think, *Now how do we tie them all together in a way where it won't be expectable?* The worst thing, for me as a moviegoer, is if I can tell you what's coming. In the story breaking department, I believe that [producer, Kevin] Feige and the [directors, Anthony and Joe] Russos and [writers, Christopher] Markus and [Stephen] McFeely do the audience justice.

What has it meant to sit in this character for so long? I can make a couple of comparisons. Not to compare myself to Charlie Chaplin, but people wanted to see

> "The worst thing for me as a moviegoer, is if I can tell you what's coming. I believe [the filmmakers] do the audience justice."

him play the tramp. He did *Monsieur Verdoux*, he did *Limelight* – he had successful forays into not just being his most beloved character. But ultimately, in his autumn years he surrendered to the will of the people and re-found his joy and his acceptance in the fact that he'd been fortunate enough to have channeled and created that character to begin with.

Tony was out there for me to begin with. But you don't think of the two separately. I think if you'd done as many of these films as I have and the first one was so definitive and game-changing – not because I'm so great, but because everybody did their job so well – what

[director, Jon] Favreau did and what Gwyneth [Paltrow] did and everybody... It's just like having a great football team, a great group of folks.

What do directors Anthony and Joe Russo bring to *Endgame*?
The funny thing is you'd always meet the next director while you were driving around on the studio lot with the director you were working with. Jon [Favreau] was the blasting cap, and so many other folks have come in and been able to carry the torch and pass it back and forth because it's a co-op of individuality and also of like-mindedness.

▶

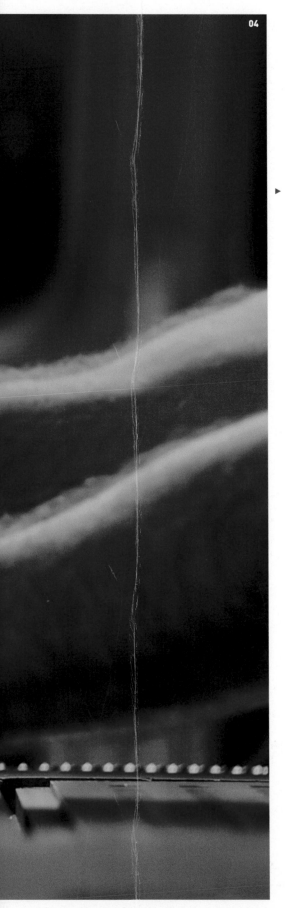

04

"I sense the best is yet to come. I'm really looking forward to how people lose their marbles over *Endgame*."

▶ Joss [Whedon] was the perfect guy for getting *Avengers* off the ground. Anthony and Joe are about the only two folks that I could imagine doing these two movies. Not just for still having the respect of the cast and crew when we were done filming, but also for not being in some other way permanently damaged by it. The physical and mental stripping of one's chi that it takes – these films are years and years and years of work. They've essentially been on a job for six or seven years now. I love them, and they love the Avengers.

Do you ever look back and see the relevance of certain parts of earlier films?
It was all there in this universe to begin with. That's why Marvel comics have always been so numinous to kids and grown-ups and people generally. There's this love for it because it speaks to the world, but it also speaks to the democratic American projected dream, which is far more complicated than that.

But there's an ideal there that's always been trying to express itself. Strangely, in some ways the best of it has been expressed in these little two-hour segments of entertainment.

What do you enjoy the most about working on Marvel Studios productions?
The memories of my co-workers, those moments and days we've had. I still remember Tony landing in the high desert in the eastern Sierras when he escapes the cave. I was buried up to my neck in sand and a storm was coming in. We only had a couple of minutes to get this take and it was like God's grace just came in and gave us the take that was in the movie.

The nice thing is, I sense the best is yet to come. I'm really looking forward to how people lose their marbles over it. This is the only film I've ever participated in where I guarantee you there's no way anybody could guess what's going to happen.

I think that there's so little mystery left in life – social media, everyone's 'TMI', and all that stuff. It's like everybody knows everything about everybody. And oftentimes you know what you're going to see before you go there. Some people even think, *Oh, we have to let people know that they're going to see what they expect to see so they can enjoy themselves.* The reason I love movies is because I love being taken on an unexpected journey. I love being surprised and thrilled and delighted and maybe sometimes taught just a little bit, a little something about myself. Ⓐ

04 Stark's shattered Iron Man helmet

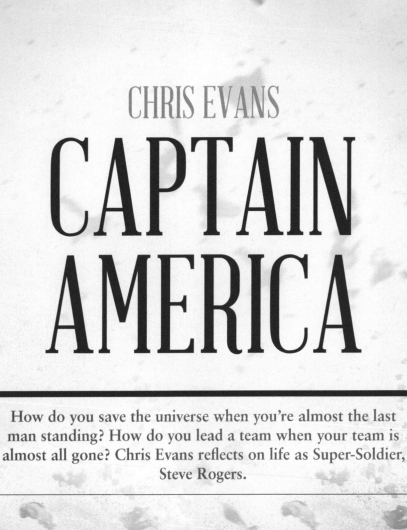

CHRIS EVANS

CAPTAIN AMERICA

How do you save the universe when you're almost the last man standing? How do you lead a team when your team is almost all gone? Chris Evans reflects on life as Super-Soldier, Steve Rogers.

01

"We had a map showing all these different storylines coming together, culminating with *Endgame.*"

Avengers: Infinity War was earth-shattering for audiences. What was your take on it?
Chris Evans: Even I was affected. I knew it was coming, and I was wiping tears away. So, that's proof right there. If you know the story and it still kind of rocks you, that's proof Marvel Studios are doing something right.

How can the team find hope after *Infinity War*?
Well, the good thing is it's always easier to build people back up after they've been broken down. So, at the beginning of this movie we see a lot of broken people. That's what Marvel Studios is great at doing. They've truly leveled us, not just literally, but morally and emotionally.

Where do we find Steve Rogers as *Endgame* begins?
He still has his back turned on things as a result of Civil War. But after Thanos completed his plan and we lost all these people, Steve's really trying to jumpstart that optimism and rediscover that loyalty to conventions bigger than himself, and to somehow stay afloat. Otherwise, it's so easy for him to just give up. But that's not in his nature; I think he knows that. It's a matter of him figuring out how to still be a leader in the face of the worst possible outcome.

It's really good writing.
I'm truly baffled by the web of stories that Marvel Studios has somehow mapped out. It's a gigantic tapestry, a collage of plots and characters that somehow all unite; there's so much connective tissue. It's hard to understand how, if you have this great *Avengers* movie, how are the Super Heroes going to have their own individual stories? But Marvel Studios do it, and it works.

Is *Avengers: Endgame* going to be an emotional experience for the audience?
Every time you think Marvel Studios have pulled everything out of the bag, you realize that they have actually saved the big stuff for this one – and rightfully so. We had a map showing all these different storylines coming together, culminating with *Endgame*. Hats off to Kevin Feige, and everyone at Marvel Studios. They really deserve all the praise.

The fact it's been handled so deftly has to be in reflection of something special.
Movies aren't easy to make. If they were easier to make, there'd be a lot more good ones. The fact that these guys not only made a few good ones, but managed to marry them all in this unbelievable tapestry, feels like an unrepeatable feat. These films are perennial. These films will last.

01 Steve holds on to the memory of Peggy Carter

02 "Some people move on, but not us. Not us." Steve dons his Captain America gear

03 A pensive Steve Rogers faces the ultimate challenge in the wake of Thanos' victory

Does *Endgame* show the Avengers' side of Thanos' story?
It's easy, when the villain is so clearly bad, to hate him. Marvel Studios have done this strange thing with Thanos where they gave him a logical point of view, in my opinion. He's a sort of masked misanthrope or something cloaked in a binary logic about the greater good. Thanos' thought process is pretty ubiquitous in politics and religion.

He's not just this evil guy. He thinks he's doing a good thing, which makes him sympathetic to some degree. [Josh] Brolin really grounds him in this kind of human way so you don't see a monster or a villain. You see a person who thinks they're doing something good.

As soon as he went too far, there's a flashback to baby Gamora.
Exactly. He has a heart in there somewhere. He thinks he's doing the right thing. That's what makes it so great. In this movie, we reveal a more sinister element to him, that it isn't this kind of selfless design for the greater good. It really is just his nasty nature.

Going back to the very start of your Marvel Studios days, did you have any idea your character would be so rich?
No, and it's tough to try and present challenges to someone who is so selfless. Steve Rogers doesn't carry around this brooding nature. It's tough to pose a problem that he can't solve, and it's tough to make him dynamic to watch when he doesn't offer up his struggle. That's what Marvel Studios have done such a great job of doing. He's always been this very austere kind of guy but has a real loyalty to institutions and to people.

Across the movies, that's slowly stripped away from him. He loses his faith in government in *Captain America: The Winter Soldier* and his friends and family in *Captain America: Civil War*. When we see him in *Avengers: Infinity War* he's just turned his back on a lot of things. In *Endgame*, he returns to that kind of sanguine, hopeful soldier/leader. ▶

"Marvel Studios know how to inject a certain pathos into everything, beyond the fights and explosions."

Was it fulfilling as an actor when his arc evolved?
Absolutely. The biggest worry is not only trying to make the guy entertaining but to make sure the series stays entertaining. I just really credit everyone over at Marvel Studios. They know these stories inside out. They're incredibly fastidious. I mean, they're fans themselves. So they've done their homework, and they know what the fans want. They know when they're coloring outside the lines. They somehow manage to stay loyal to the source material but also give Steve Rogers enough challenges to keep him interesting enough to have audiences want him coming back.

What was it like building up chemistry with Robert Downey Jr.?
It's beyond necessary. Marvel Studios know how to inject a certain amount of pathos into everything, beyond the fights and explosions. I think that's par for the course for any big budget studio movie where you have a lot of action. You want to make sure you care about the characters. You want to make sure you're emotionally invested and that you're sympathetic and that you identify with a character's humanity. Marvel Studios have managed to take these larger than life characters and find ways for audiences, who maybe don't live larger than life lives, to connect, identify, and sympathize with them.

Was the spark with him instant?
It's not hard with Downey. He's a very affable guy, and I think he really understood the weight of the responsibility with these movies. He understood that when one person succeeds, we all succeed. So he really went out of his way to help us find our footing, not just in the *Avengers* films but in our own individual franchise movies as well. Even when he wasn't on set, I still felt his support.

In the beginning that was really necessary for me. I think I would have struggled quite a bit without it. When you meet him he's got a real energy about him. There's a real gravity that he brings. As a result, he really helped the actors, who, like [Chris] Hemsworth and myself, had done things before these movies, but nothing as big. He put everyone on his back and made sure everyone was swimming in the same direction. Before we knew it, we were like a crew team. Everyone was rowing in rhythm, and we were flying!

04 A reflective moment for Steve Rogers

05 Chris Evans and Robert Downey Jr consult with director Joe Russo

04

▶

06

You must have to be serious about your craft to keep up with him?

He's so good at what he does, sometimes you just want to get out of the way. You don't want to get in there and start micromanaging. If he changes a scene in a certain way, I just trust him. He instinctively knows what's good.

Tell us about the directors, Anthony and Joe Russo...

I remember them on the first couple of days on *The Winter Soldier*. They really felt like the new kids in the playground and it's intimidating because they were walking into a playground where we play games well, and they're the new guy, and what are they going to bring? They paid their dues in the way you have to pay your dues. *The Winter Soldier* came out so well. They're

true cinephiles. They know so much about movies. Their directing style is really connected to that knowledge because they can reference other things in a way that I've not seen other directors do. Right away you can understand what they're looking to convey with the scene. They're also incredibly personable guys. So, their attitude breeds a sense of lightness on set, which makes everyone feel like it's a game.

Were you surprised with how well *The Winter Soldier* turned out?

No, because the Russo Brothers would express what they wanted the movie to be in its entirety and what they saw each scene as. Then when you see it, it's exactly what they wanted. I've been in plenty of movies where they

"The Russo brothers are true cinephiles. They know so much about movies... They're also incredibly personable guys."

say one thing on set, but when you see the final product, it's not what you'd talked about. On this, everything they said they were going to do they delivered on.

What makes producer Kevin Feige so special?
I wish I knew everything that went into the prep stages of a film. It would be easier to question whether it really was all his handiwork that makes these movies a success if he didn't have such an unblemished record. You can see plenty of studio heads who have one giant success and then one complete dud, and then justify that by saying that there's a lot of moving pieces to a movie. For some reason, Kevin is batting a thousand. If he's the only common denominator across all of these films, there's your proof. ⒶⓋ

06 Black Widow joins Captain America: "We lost. All of us. We lost friends. We lost family. We lost a part of ourselves. This is the fight of our lives."

SCARLETT JOHANSSON
BLACK WIDOW

A highly-trained former agent of S.H.I.E.L.D., Natasha Romanoff first appea
in Marvel Studios' *Iron Man 2*. It's been a long journey to Marvel Studios
Avengers: Endgame for Scarlett Johansson...

Black Widow has had a fascinating character arc so far. Was this planned from the start?
Scarlett Johansson: When I did *Iron Man 2,* I didn't know if audiences would accept my interpretation of this character. While I knew there were many different dramatic directions that we could go in and different parts of the character that we could reveal, at that point it was just an introduction to this character. It wasn't until the first *Avengers* movie that I got to work with Joss Whedon and really work on Natasha's characterization and develop her backstory.

Have Natasha's life experiences given her a different outlook to her fellow Avengers?
I think Natasha is a little bit different than other Super Heroes, because she has a different moral compass to her fellow Avengers, even Captain America.

Natasha understands that there's a balance between dark and light in the world, and she understands the sacrifice you have to make on either side in order to have balance. That might not be a reality that some of the other characters are willing to swallow. I don't think she has to have the same mindset as her fellow heroes in order to work alongside them, though – she just looks at the world in a different way.

> "I really love Natasha. I love that she is constantly evolving."

Is she the voice of reason in the team?
Yeah, I think she doesn't really take things personallyShe just thinks of things in a very strategic way. She's just very pragmatic.

Do you see Black Widow as a role model?
I really love Natasha. I love that she is constantly evolving. She doesn't get stuck on things. She's just continuously moving forward. She doesn't dwell on regrets or the past, even though those things may haunt her sometimes.

She really doesn't get stuck in that syrupy sweet nostalgia. I think that's something that actually is very

inspiring about her. If that can inspire children to be risk takers, I think that's cool.

Black Widow is a highly physical role. Have you enjoyed that side of filming?
I've been so fortunate to build a relationship with Heidi Moneymaker, my stunt double, who's an incredible athlete and an inspiring person. I've been so fortunate to be able to build the physicality of the character with her from the very beginning, in *Iron Man 2*. We really got to play with the balletic quality of the character, her gymnastic background, which Heidi has 16 years of experience in.

01 Black Widow
▶ takes aim

"Natasha has a very graceful way of fighting and I think she really enjoys the physicality of it."

It's been awesome to be able to push Natasha's abilities forward as much as we can. We still have those signature moves, which are always fun to break out. The audience loves that stuff too, because it just makes them feel like they know the character by the way she moves.

Was it important for her to have a different fighting style compared to the other Avengers?
Natasha has a very graceful way of fighting and I think she really enjoys the physicality of it! There's a playfulness about it and no matter what's going on for her emotionally or how high the stakes are, when she goes into battle, she's ready for it. She loves the adrenaline.

Is the action as fun to film as it is to watch?
Yeah, they are fun to shoot. Doing these films gave me the gift of wellness and awareness of my own body. When I started out on *Iron Man 2*, I was 22 or 23. I wasn't athletic at all. I had no history in sports. I'd barely set foot in a gym. So, it was a big deal to dive into working out twice a day and doing stunt and

02

weapons training, and all kinds of strategic training. I've learned skills that I am incredibly thankful to have. Also, I get to be in shape for my job, so I feel extremely lucky!

Was making *Avengers: Infinity War* an emotional experience for you?
The devastation was very palpable on set, which is why I think it feels that way when you watch it on screen. It really felt like we were doing something extraordinary.

I often looked around the set at my fellow castmembers and it was like, *Here we are again! The original gang back together.* We've all had different experiences: some of us have had kids and had relationships that were assembled, then disassembled. We've done all kinds of

stuff with our careers, our families, and everybody in the crew as well. It does feel emotional.

Is the camaraderie real between the actors?
It's crazy looking back on it. Chris Evans and I have made seven movies together. We've known each other since I was 17. Mark Ruffalo and I have known each other forever. All of us have known each other for ten years. We've spent so much time together and gone through so much together. We actually just really enjoy being together.

Are the small character moments important?
I think the human element is what people love so much about the original comic books. They love the intricacies of the relationships and these heavy character themes ▶

03

"I think the human element is what people love so much about the original comic books."

and the weight of responsibility, remorse, guilt, and then determination. What drives the action is the character. We have to have that stuff. Otherwise, it would just be an empty experience.

03 Natasha tracks down Clint Barton in Japan

04 Scarlett Johansson as Black Widow

Does the scope of *Avengers: Endgame* top *Infinity War?*
I had the opportunity to see some of the movie, but I actually stopped watching because I wanted to be surprised like everybody else!

I think what makes *Endgame* different is that there's a lot of space for our characters to reflect. You'll see the reasoning behind the decisions that we make. It's unusual in this genre to have all of these special, meaningful moments given the space that they deserve while still moving the story along. It is a feat of editing and storytelling that I think is unprecedented.

What are the qualities that have helped Kevin Feige make such a success of the Marvel Studios movies?
He's so consistent and he's always surprising. He's incredibly open minded and really sensitive and deeply caring. He's funny and shy, but also very brave and confident. I think he's just a really multifaceted person and he's good with people.

I trust Kevin. He's never let me down. In this industry – and in life in general – that's such a rare quality. He has always been so reliable and he really cares about getting these movies done in the right way. Ⓐ

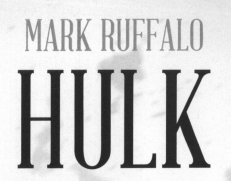

MARK RUFFALO
HULK

For Mark Ruffalo, playing Bruce Banner and Hulk, from Marvel Studios' *The Avengers* onward, has afforded the actor the opportunity to portray a character that has undergone constant change – and not just from man to monster. It's a twisting trajectory that reaches its apex with Marvel Studios' *Avengers: Endgame*.

01

What were your thoughts on *Avengers: Infinity War*?

Mark Ruffalo: I was surprised: I was really blown away by how powerful it was, and how culturally powerful it was. I saw it with my son and a bunch of his friends in a little post-industrial town up in mid-Connecticut, filled with working-class people. I was in disguise. I'd never seen a reaction like that after a movie. People were screaming and yelling. A kid took off his shirt and jumped up on the chairs, saying, "I'm gonna riot! This is bull!" People were arguing about what the ending meant, people were crying… It was profound. I just think it's such a great thing to be part of.

How has it been for you to get to evolve this character over the course of the various movies?

Part of why I became an actor is because it's always changing – I don't have to do the same thing over and over again. Luckily, Banner has had this kind of crazy trajectory. People grow over the course of 10 years, and I think it's cool that the character does. So, for me, it's been really challenging, and exciting, and often times crushing trying to make all that work and keep it interesting for myself and for the audiences.

What do you enjoy most about making films with Marvel Studios?

Honestly, I'd say the people. We've all grown up together, and had this wonderful experience together, and started families, or got married, or got divorced. It's been a long time with this group of wildly different people, with different personalities, different backgrounds, and different interests. An actor's essential journey is really like a vagabond. It's transient. You're alone. You don't see people very often. This was totally different than that. We made this beautiful family together. I'm actually really moved by it.

You've wound up with real friendships in real life.

We are as much like the Avengers in real life as what you see on the big screen – as different from one another and as beautiful together as a single organism.

Do you think Bruce Banner's scientific background has been a positive influence on the younger fans?

It's amazing the impact that these movies have had culturally. The Avengers are the good guys – they fight for what's good, and they use science, they use reason, and they are nerds. We've lifted up this whole part of being a young person, and had a hand in the conversation about the moral center of the culture, turned young people on to the idea of science. I hold science in very high regard.

Is it gratifying to see more female Super Heroes on screen now?

The amazing thing about Marvel Studios is they have their hand on the pulse of the culture, and I would say they are even a bit of a leader of where we are, where we were, and where we're going. What's pretty astounding about Marvel Studios is how quickly, culturally, they've accepted these changes and these challenges of a quality of decency and inclusion. It's a much better universe because of it. To be part of that makes me so proud – and also, to see that it's so successful and it's what people want. That's borne out by movie tickets and audience reaction. It's quantifiable.

Which Super Hero does Kevin Feige embody?

Kevin is like Vision, because he has vision. He has a *lot* of vision, clearly! Ⓐ

01 Banner surveys the missing heroes

02 The Hulk, suited up and ready to join the fight

"We are as much like the Avengers in real life as what you see on the big screen."

Marvel Studios' *Avengers: Infinity War*

03 The Hulk, last seen aboard the Sanctuary II. (Marvel Studios' *Avengers: Infinity War*)

04 The Hulk takes on Thanos in brutal battle that ends badly for Hulk. (Marvel Studios' *Avengers: Infinity War*)

05 The Mad Titan easily stops the usually unstoppable Hulk. (Marvel Studios' *Avengers: Infinity War*)

06 Hulk smashed! (Marvel Studios' *Avengers: Infinity War*)

07 Saved by Heimdall. (Marvel Studios' *Avengers: Infinity War*)

Marvel Studios' *Avengers: Infinity War*

05

Marvel Studios' *Avengers: Infinity War*

06

Marvel Studios' *Avengers: Infinity War*

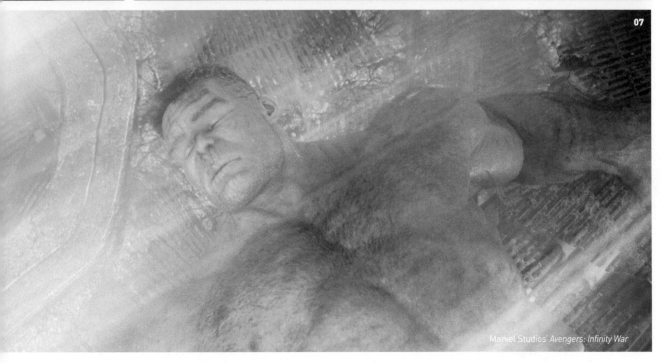

07

Marvel Studios' *Avengers: Infinity War*

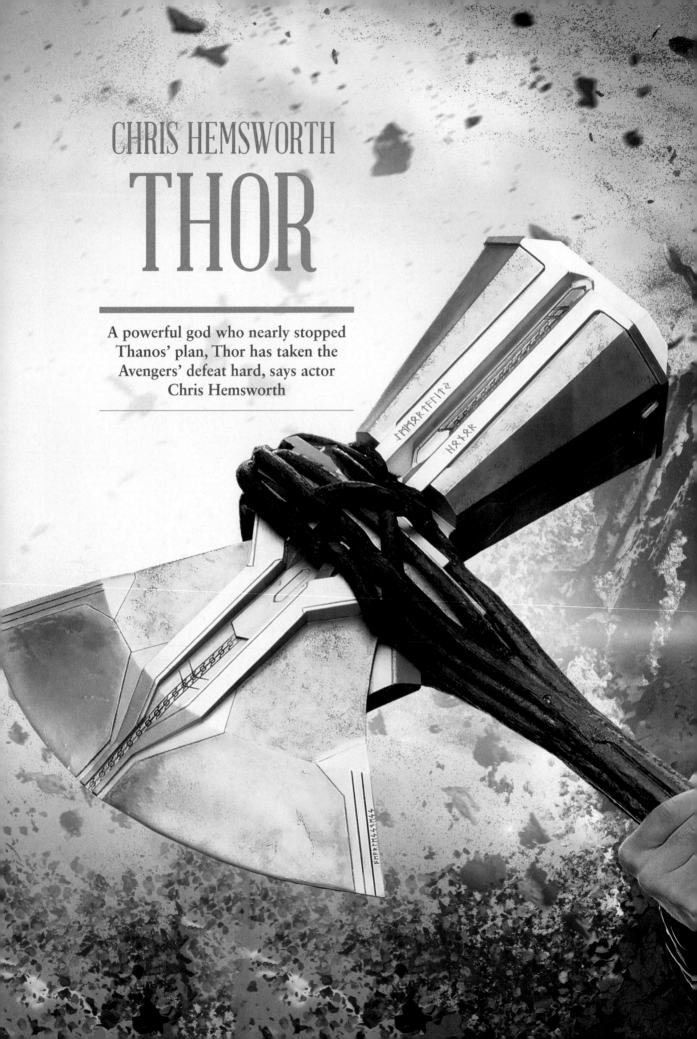

CHRIS HEMSWORTH
THOR

A powerful god who nearly stopped
Thanos' plan, Thor has taken the
Avengers' defeat hard, says actor
Chris Hemsworth

01

Where is Thor at as *Endgame* starts?

Chris Hemsworth: If *Thor: Ragnarok* showed Thor at his wackiest and *Infinity War* showed Thor at his best, *Avengers: Endgame* shows Thor at his worst. Emotionally and physically, every aspect of him is broken, lost, and uncertain.

That was a whole new journey for him and it felt like I was playing a completely different character. I was even freer than I'd ever felt before because there are no rules at this point. There was a real opportunity to swing for the fences. It was so much fun.

If I had have been given this version of Thor to play earlier, I think I would've dropped the ball in a big way. So it has happened at a perfect time for my development as a human being and an actor. I was able to tap into some interesting things that I hadn't looked at before, and that was a great experience. I loved it.

Has playing the different facets of the character made playing a Super Hero more interesting for you?

I couldn't be happier with being able to experiment each time. After *Thor: Ragnarok* I thought we'd hit the ceiling with it, but Marvel Studios had yet another version of the character and now there is another version. I feel beyond lucky to be able to tie it all up. Creatively it was so satisfying. I really felt flat-footed at times with the character, so to be able to embark on a whole different journey was awesome.

How high are the stakes in *Avengers: Endgame*?

I think it's the darkest film in the series in some ways, but it's the wackiest in other ways. It feels like there's a real drama at its core – it's a small, indie, character-driven drama on one hand. It's also the most expensive, visually stunning, smorgasbord effects-driven film you could ever imagine!

I don't know how Marvel Studios managed to pull it off. But they have, and I take my hat off to them. Ⓐ

01 Hemsworth plays his once heroic character as "broken, lost, and uncertain"

"If I had been given this version of Thor to play earlier, I think I would've dropped the ball in a big way."

02

02 Hemsworth feels that, "there's a real drama at [*Endgame*'s] core"

Marvel Studios' *Avengers' Infinity War*

Marvel Studios' *Avengers' Infinity War*

03 Thor joins the battle in Wakanda

04 The God of Thunder weilds his newly acquired weapon, Stormbreaker

05 Chris Hemsworth as Thor

03

04

05

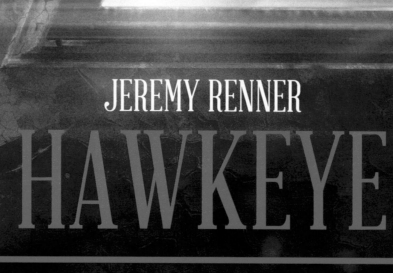

JEREMY RENNER

HAWKEYE

Marvel Studios' *Avengers: Endgame* presents a new take on
Hawkeye aka Clint Barton...

01

Is Hawkeye a fun character to play?
Jeremy Renner: It was something I dreamed of for a long time. There's a lot of value and a lot at stake for him. I couldn't have been more excited that that idea was coming. The Russos slipped that idea to me early on and I just couldn't be more excited to go work with them and see what else they would come up with. There are always physical challenges in these movies, but there are more emotional challenges in *Avengers: Endgame*.

I think it's a great way to end the journey thus far for the character where he's kind of transgressed and grown and formed relationships with Black Widow, amongst the others.

Did you do new training?
It's something I had to pick up quickly because I was still healing from breaking my arms on a previous film. There was some physical adversity Clint had to deal with. I was glad he turned into Ronin because I couldn't hold the bow anyway! Ronin uses throwing stars and all these other fun, cool toys instead, I had to learn how to use them quickly with our great stunt team.

Where is Clint at with his relationships?
There's a lot of humanity to Clint because he's a boots-on-the-ground kind of guy. He doesn't have any super powers, just a very strong will and a high skill set. There's a wonderful grounding relationship with Black Widow. It's really quite beautiful, and I think it's expressed well in *Avengers: Endgame*. Clint and Natasha have a big connection which continues to deepen. That was really wonderful because it's kind of where we started. The Hawkeye/Widow relationship is one of the most important amongst the Avengers for Clint.

Scarlett Witch had also became a very important character to him – he was more like a father figure for her. All those relationships have grown through this episodic type of film-making.

Is it hard to keep track of what is going on with all of the characters in a film of this scale?
In *Civil War* that happened a lot during the big battle in the airport. I always had to keep check on who was who: *Do I know this person? Do I not know this person? Do I like them?* I always had to keep some truth to it.

In *Endgame*, there are some epic battles that are just out of control.

> "I had to pick up [training] quickly because I was still healing from breaking my arms on a previous film."

02

01 Hawkeye is back and ready to fight in Marvel Studios' *Avengers: Endgame*

02 Barton prepares for combat on the streets of Japan

PEPPER POTTS

She's been there since the very first installment of the Marvel Cinematic Universe, but had no idea she was actually making history. Gwyneth Paltrow reflects on a decade of Pepper Potts.

Marvel Studios' *Iron Man 2*

You've been there since the very beginning of the Marvel Cinematic Universe. Has it been fun to track Pepper's evolution?

Gwyneth Paltrow: It's interesting. Pepper and I have taken a very similar parallel journey in a lot of ways. In the first *Iron Man* movie, she was in a much different place in her life. She's really come into her own throughout the course of the movies as a leader. In some ways, I caught up to her, and she caught up to me. I hold Pepper very close to my heart. She's certainly the character that I have played the longest. She's been in my life for over 10 years. I think she's an incredible person. I really actually have a lot of love for Pepper.

How do your children feel about having a comic book hero for a mom?

My son Moses and my stepson Brody came to the *Infinity War* premiere with me. They were my dates and they loved it! Oh my God, they think it's amazing. My kids went to summer camp this year and my son said, 'Is it okay that people in my cabin know that you're Pepper Potts? 'Cause they know that you're Pepper Potts.' I was like, 'It's okay with me if it's okay with you.' I think they're proud. I think that Marvel Studios has really come to represent something profound for these kids. The stories are so mythological and archetypal which resonates so well with the children.

They feel very empowered watching these films. When I saw *Black Panther*, I loved it, and they loved it. They're just regular kids and they can't wait for the next Marvel Studios movie to come out.

How do you feel about Marvel Studios catching up to what's happened in society?

I think it sort of happened in tandem when you think about it. We have culturally gotten to a place where women are demanding equality. That's in the workplace, whether you're in a Super Hero costume or an office job. There's a very powerful theme running through the culture right now.

Marvel Studios are doing a great job of amplifying that in the films and representing that properly. They've listened to where we are. They've been responsive, and that's a beautiful thing.

01 Tony and Pepper's marriage banter in New York is rudely interrupted in Marvel Studios' *Avengers: Infinity War*

"Robert Downey Jr is my co-star, both when we are on set together and off."

What's your favorite part about working with Robert Downey Jr?

Robert is my co-star, both when we're on set together and off. He is so surprising. You never know what he's going to do, and so he makes the day really fun and very dynamic. He's just incredible to play with.

Has he always been like that?

I was thinking back to the first *Iron Man* movie where we just improvised the whole thing basically on the spot. Robert has really taught me a lot about improvisation. He's such a unique and brilliant actor. And to work with him really keeps you on your toes and keeps the creative spirit alive.

You're now firm friends with him off-screen as well, aren't you?

Of course! Personally, he's really become a brother to me. Robert's one of my best friends. He's someone that I will see all the time even when we're not working. I'm really happy he convinced me to do that first *Iron Man* movie 10 years ago, because if it wasn't for him pushing me to do it, I don't think I would have done it. So, I'm really grateful to him because, here I am! Ⓐ

DON CHEADLE
WAR MACHINE

Marvel Studios 'Avengers: Infinity War saw a rehabilitated Colonel James Rhodes defy General Ross in order to stand with the Avengers against the threat of Thanos. Now, in Marvel Studios' *Avengers: Endgame*, Rhodey faces his greatest test yet, as Don Cheadle reveals.

How did you feel when you finally saw Avengers: Infinity War?

Don Cheadle: Well, I couldn't have imagined how far this would come from 10 years ago. I really never envisioned what it would be like to have so many people from the Marvel Cinematic Universe all together on one set, in one story – how the storylines complement each other and how they affect one another. It's really an awesome achievement. That's a testament to Kevin Feige [Marvel Studios President] and everybody at Marvel Studios for keeping this mythology together – finding ways to create storylines that work for the comics, but at the same time work in concert with what we're trying to do as a live action film.

What an we expect to see from James Rhodes/War Machine in Avengers: Endgame?

We always want to see our characters do more than we sometimes get the opportunity to do. But I think in *Endgame*, we really get to see a lot of dimensions of Rhodey, of him getting back on his feet – literally, emotionally and physically – after his trials and tribulations and everything that he's been through. So, I've had a nice arc in this character run. It's been fun.

What was it like to work with so many fellow A-list actors on this movie?

That's the really incredible part of it. Similar to the day that we all took the [Marvel Studios 10th anniversary] photograph, there were so many people whose work we've admired over the years. To get to meet these people, then to get to play with them and have that moment cemented on film forever is kind of special.

They do such a good job of keeping a lot of stuff secret that we get to still be surprised when we're filming and seeing who's there. We all check in with each other to understand what's happening!

Is it hard to keep track of your character when you're operating under so much secrecy?

That's why it's incumbent upon Joe and Anthony [Russo] to really keep us aware of where we're coming from, where we're headed, and what the stakes are. We are often reminding each other. Sometimes they'll forget because they've been working on this franchise forever, too. This has been an epic journey for them as well. We have to remind each other sometimes – like, "Wait a minute, we played that beat in this way." ▶

01

"In *Endgame*, we get to see a lot of dimensions of Rhodey..."

Marvel Studios' *Avengers: Infinity War*

"The scope of this thing is immense and huge, but from the success of the first film, it's something the fans clearly want."

It can be a little schizophrenic, but that has been the process from the beginning. When you're working on a movie that has so many effects and so many storylines happening, you always have to go back to the basics and build it – reverse-engineer where you have to get to.

For all the spectacle of Avengers: Endgame, there are also many elements that help to ground the film.
That's why these movies pay off: there's the grandeur, and then there'll be very intimate scenes. It plays between that pretty quickly. You can have big comedic moments, and then very, very strong dramatic moments and huge fantastical sets. That's something that's rare and amazing.

That said, the movie certainly doesn't stint on spectacle…
The scope of this thing is immense and huge, but from the success of the first film, it's something that the fans clearly want. They understand what they're coming to, and I think the movies keep delivering it.

What do you take from this whole experience?
We've become these nuclear families: we go away, we have our own things that we do in disparate parts of the world, then we come back and have these concentrated, intense moments together. It has been a very interesting 10 years! It's amazing and rare to work on something that's not a TV series, or a long-running play, but a movie franchise in which we keep coming back to explore these characters. It's very interesting in that aspect. Ⓐ

01 Don Cheadle as Colonel James Rhodes

02 War Machine and Ant-Man

03 War Machine in Wakanda (Marvel Studios' *Avengers: Infinity War*)

04 War Machine, a formidable Stark-armored warrior

Marvel Studios' *Avengers: Infinity War*

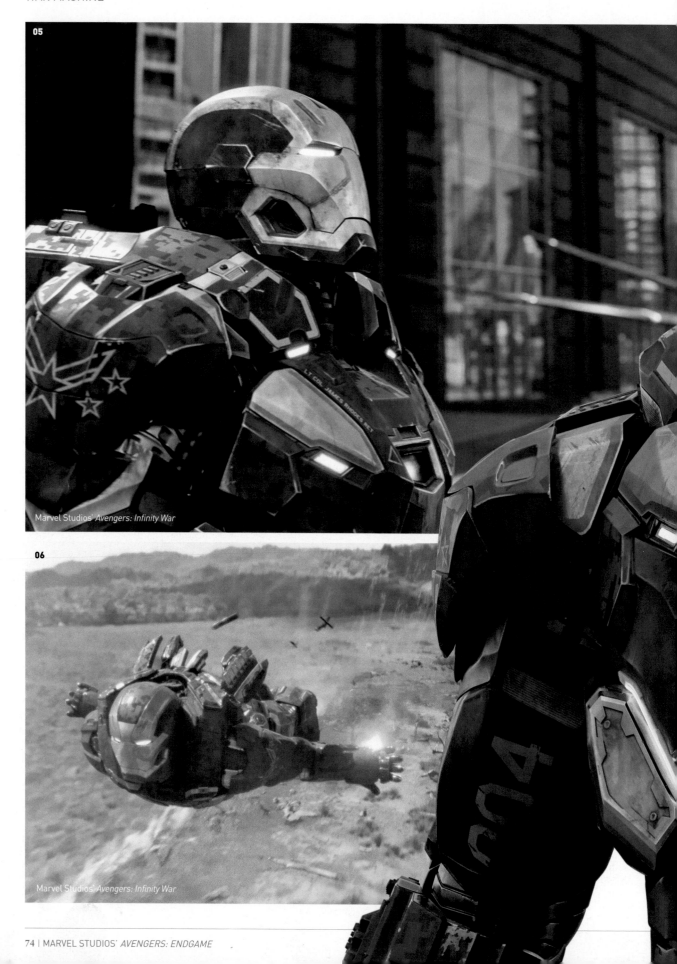

05

Marvel Studios' *Avengers: Infinity War*

06

Marvel Studios' *Avengers: Infinity War*

05 War Machine, made his debut in 2010's *Iron Man 2*

06 Rhodes surveys the carnage in Wakanda during the closing moments of Marvel Studios' *Avengers: Infinity War*

07 War Machine soars into action over the Wakandan battlefield (Marvel Studios' *Avengers: Infinity War*)

Marvel Studios' *Avengers: Infinity War*

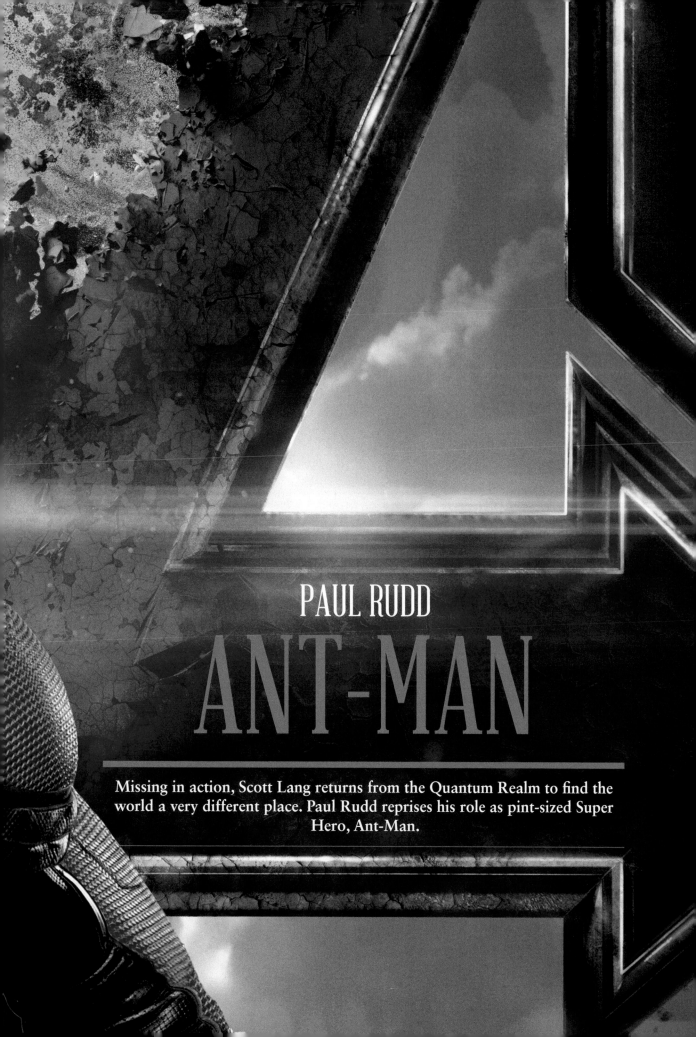

PAUL RUDD

ANT-MAN

Missing in action, Scott Lang returns from the Quantum Realm to find the world a very different place. Paul Rudd reprises his role as pint-sized Super Hero, Ant-Man.

What is it like to work with all the other Marvel characters?

Paul Rudd: It's cool to talk to everybody. I notice other people are on set just watching because there is this feeling that this is a pretty cool thing to be a part of. It's amazing to see it in person.

Was there an actor you were looking forward to working with the most?

It's been interesting for me in the last few years to become a character in this world. I still feel a part of it, but I'm also thinking, *What am I doing in this universe?* It was so different to anything I really expected. I really enjoy it. I like all the people involved in the production. I like playing this part, and I have enjoyed the creative process of working on these films and hopefully I will continue to enjoy it. But it's been somewhat of a surreal chapter in my life. Every job is surreal in its own way, but this is kind of a prolonged stretch.

I was standing around today in my Ant-Man suit and I just started laughing. I'm a grown-up. How did this happen?

How have you settled into your role?

There's something about the way that Marvel Studios make their films which makes it unlike any other place I've ever worked at. They really care about their films and work hard to make them inventive and emotional. The way they go about doing that is different, and the way they make their films is different. I have learned to trust their process and I find it very exciting to work that way. So the process is no longer new to me, definitely.

I feel as if I understand the machine behind it all a little bit more, just because I have more familiarity with the people that are involved and the studio itself. I've been to the offices and spent time there. My relationship with the studio and the people has grown. That's one thing that I feel has changed a bit just because of time. It's the same with my relationship with the other Avengers.

In *Civil War* I showed up and I had already filmed *Ant-Man*, but this was the first time I saw the other Super Heroes. Now I feel as if I've been to this party before. I feel like I didn't just get an invitation on a fluke.

How has Scott Lang grown from the first *Ant-Man*?

In the first *Ant-Man* film we had this whole new world for this character who was trying to wrap his brain around the idea that he could talk to ants and he could ▶

"I was standing around today in my Ant-Man suit and I just started laughing!"

01 Paul Rudd as "everyman" Super Hero, Ant-Man

02

03

Marvel Studios' *Ant-Man and The Wasp*

"My relationship with the studio and the people has grown.... It's the same with my relationship with the other Avengers."

Marvel Studios' *Ant-Man and The Wasp*

▶ shrink. Then we fast forward to *Civil War* and it's like, *Whoa! Here they all are!* There's kind of a wide-eyed quality to Scott.

Now there's a bit more. I don't think that he's freaked out by the technology, but he still feels the threat of it. *Wait a minute, you mean outer space? People are in outer space?* He still has this quality of being an everyman looking in on this world that people relate to with this character.

He's much like me, being a part of the group. Scott Lang has accepted his role as Ant-Man. He's willing to do what he needs to do for the sake of the world and the people that he loves.

Are there any new alliances or relationships for Ant-Man in *Avengers: Endgame*?
I got to meet Thor! That was something we filmed. I'm assuming it'll make the movie. I don't know. It was one of those things. I said, "Hi, I'm Scott." And he said, "I'm Thor."

I have some more actual exchanges with people, such as Hulk and War Machine.

Why have fans embraced this Marvel universe?
Comic books have had a serious fan base for many ▶

04

Marvel Studios' *Ant-Man and The Wasp*

decades. Way before these movies were being made. People have a real love for these characters. When Stan Lee walked on set you felt the importance of what this man created. You look around the set and you can say, "He made that up. He made that up. He made that up." My whole life, I've known these characters, even if I didn't read the comics. There's something about these Super Heroes that is timeless. They exhibit all the qualities that we wish we had. They also have their flaws, and we recognize those qualities that we do actually have - and that's what makes them relatable.

What have been the high points, so far, in playing Scott Lang ?
The thing that I really think is just the coolest part is that kids sometimes visit the set. We had some kids from the Make A Wish Foundation or some other kids that are fanatics about these movies. For a kid to come on set and see all of this, it's the best.

It's the best thing to be a part of something where you have that kind of effect on a kid. I have found that to be the coolest part about this job.

What will audiences enjoy about this film?
Over the last ten years audiences have really gotten to know these characters. They knew the characters before the movies, but now they really associate these actors

05 Scott Lang arrives at the Avengers' compound

06 Lang fully suited as Ant-Man

> "When Stan Lee walked on set, you felt the importance of what this man created."

with these characters. A generation of people have grown up with them. So I think that there's something very emotional about all of this.

What do the Russo brothers bring to these films?
They shoot with a real efficiency. It's a quality you want in a director. They both have it. Sometimes it'll be Joe that comes and says something. Sometimes it'll be Anthony.

Is your son impressed that his dad is a Super Hero?
My son only cares about football, music and sports. I think he always liked this idea that I was a part of the Marvel Cinematic Universe, but he still thinks Robert Downey Jr. is way cooler than I am. And he's right! ⓐ

KAREN GILLAN

NEBULA

Being the daughter of the tyrannical Thanos has not spared Nebula from his brutality, but now is the time to fight back says actress Karen Gillan.

01

Nebula really suffered in *Avengers: Infinity War*. Did that make you like her more?
Karen Gillan: I love my character in particular because of the emotional baggage that she comes with. She suffers such abuse from her father, Thanos, who happens to be the ultimate Marvel Super Villain. We're all fighting against him, and Nebula has an explosion of emotions because of her past and what she experienced with him. The whole thing is a very emotional, bitter, maybe weirdly cathartic experience for her.

What has Josh Brolin's performance brought to the dynamic between Thanos and Nebula?
I love the relationship between Nebula and Thanos, even just on the page between the characters. I feel so lucky that such an incredible actor is playing him. Josh Brolin is one of the best actors out there. Whenever I'm acting opposite him he makes it really easy for me to play my character because he's playing his so well. He's so sinister. He brings a little bit of humanity to a character that could potentially be a little one-dimensional. Thanos could just be a scary villain, but she's not that – he's *so* much worse than that and *so* much more. It's just a little unsettling in the best possible way.

What has been your favorite part of this film-making process?
Working on a movie of this scale is so exciting because no expense is spared. The effects are incredible and the sets are awe-inspiring. The whole thing is on a gigantic scale. Ultimately what it boils down to for me is character, and I love my character so much. I think about her all the time! I know that sounds weird, but her motivations and her agendas are so clear, and that makes it really easy to play. *Avengers: Infinity War* has all of these exciting tropes of a big blockbuster movie, but ultimately it always boils down to how compelling the characters are.

How has the camaraderie been during filming?
Hanging out with everyone on the set is one of the best parts of this job because there is this feeling of being in a large extended family. And now I get to hang out with all of my cousins too. It's fun! We can eat lunch together! Marvel Studios carve out enough time for us to do that. There's a lot of socializing that goes on while we're in costume and makeup, which is just absurd to look at! Ⓐ

"The whole thing is a very emotional, bitter, maybe weirdly cathartic experience for her."

02

Marvel Studios' *Avengers: Infinity War*

JUDIANNA MAKOVSKY, COSTUME DESIGNER

Can you talk about Nebula's new look?
Judianna Makovsky (Costume Designer): Originally we all wanted her to stay in the same costume because the directors liked the one from *Guardians*. However, I thought that made no sense – I didn't see why she would stay in the Ravagers costume. So I decided on another costume and showed it to the team, and they agreed. Her character becomes much more part of the Marvel family, and is not such an outcast. She's sort of Ravager-like, but her costume doesn't have the red coloring from the *Guardians* movie.

What was Karen Gillan's reaction to her new costume?
I showed her a sketch and she loved it. Then we just made it and had several fittings to get it to fit well. It was a late decision to make a whole new costume, so there weren't as many fittings as we'd normally do. I always try and show the actors sketches beforehand. There are certain actors that you work very closely with, like Robert Downey Jr. There are certain costumes where you know what they will look like, such as Captain America's. We work closely with the actors because it has to look good on them and the sketches will change. A sketch is just a sketch, but everything changes in a fitting. With Nebula, I'd worked with Karen before and know her character very well, so it was really fun to do something new. Ⓐ

01 Nebula dons her new gear as she plays a key role in Marvel Studios' *Avengers: Endgame*

02 Nebula and Gamora aboard Thanos' ship

03 Stunning production artwork by Alexander Mandradjiev
used to create the torture sequence from *Avengers: Infinity War*

EXECUTIVE ACTIONS

As Co-President of Marvel Studios, Louis D'Esposito has been a driving force in the Marvel Cinematic Universe from its earliest days. Joining him as an Executive Producer on Marvel Studios' *Avengers: Endgame* is Trinh Tran, whose meteoric rise from assistant on the MCU's earliest films to Executive Producer on Marvel Studios' *Avengers: Infinity War* and Marvel Studios' *Avengers: Endgame* has mirrored that of Marvel Studios itself.

Trinh, what are your feelings as you reflect on the whole experience of *Avengers: Infinity War* and *Endgame*, and the journey to these films?

Trinh Tran: It was definitely a journey, and at first it was overwhelming. But I knew that it was a big challenge, and I wasn't ever going to say no to that. At one point I thought Kevin [Feige] was crazy: you're going to put me in this position and give me this opportunity, which is amazing; but also, it's two of the biggest movies that Marvel Studios has ever made. So, to trust me with that is an amazing feeling.

Also, to be a part of it, and to take the journey with the Russo brothers and [writers Chris] Markus and [Steve] McFeely and the rest of the crew for the year and a half that we were in Atlanta shooting the two movies; and then seeing it at the end, watching it with everybody at the premiere – where, for some people, it was the first time that they had ever seen it – it was a pretty overwhelming feeling. Altogether it was amazing.

Louis, were you surprised by the reaction to *Infinity War*, especially the ending?

Louis D'Esposito: Well, we weren't sure what the response was going to be. How often does the villain win in such a resounding way that you lose approximately half of your Super Heroes and half of the living creatures in the universe?

So, we weren't quite sure. We thought [the audience] might revolt on us. But I think it was a mixed bag: some people hated it but loved it at the same time; some people loved it because they knew there was another *Avengers* movie coming out to see how this all wrapped up. But the common denominator through it all is that people were really moved by it: Marvel Studios has gone in completely another direction and has done something different. The villain wins. The heroes lose. Now what happens?

It's certainly not your typical Super Hero movie ending...

TT: We knew going in that we had to really be meticulous about who we were going to choose to be blipped out. It was a very conscientious choice for each of the characters, and I was a little scared in terms of, "Oh my gosh, how are [the actors] going to react to this, especially [when it's] their characters? They've been with us for several movies." But I think everybody was really into the fact that this is the first time that Marvel Studios has made a movie where our villain actually wins at the end. Our heroes were brutally defeated by Thanos.

So it was very exciting to take that leap and do something different, and then to have audiences embrace that at the end. When they watched the movie, it was bittersweet. It was overwhelming in the sense that this was the first time our heroes were defeated this way, and some of our characters didn't make it at the end. But in a good way it was a change, in that the audience was pretty surprised that we actually took that challenge. I love that people embraced that.

▶

Was it hard to decide which characters to blip out at the end of *Infinity War*?

TT: There is a reason why we kept specific characters at the end of *Infinity War* and why they survived, because we wanted the original Avengers in this film to really cope and deal with what they're going through. These are the original Avengers that have gone through the journey with us for the last how many films. We wanted to really explore their state of mind after what Thanos did to them. To be able to have the Avengers come together, reunite, and really join forces to stop the biggest, baddest villain that we've ever had – that's a pretty good feeling.

There was an incredibly emotional reaction by the audience to the end of *Infinity War*. To what do you attribute that?

TT: I think the small, little character moments are very important in our Marvel Studios movies. Audiences have invested in these characters for the last 10 years; with *Endgame*, it will be 22 movies that we've done. Over the years, audiences have grown to love all these characters. I think what audiences are embracing are all the character moments that we've invested in the stories.

LD: They've grown to love these characters over a 10-year period. The other thing I think that was really important is that we had a villain that was also loved. Josh Brolin's performance as Thanos is truly remarkable. It's a computer generated character, but we motion-captured him, and his performance absolutely comes through. He is a villain that has a clear goal, that is passionate about what he's going to do, and believes in what he's going to do so much so that he has to kill someone he loves, his daughter Gamora.

Thanos has been coming since the first *Avengers* movie in 2012. We've been building up the sense of anticipation for him to face our heroes for a very long time. The combination of all our heroes getting together – especially right after *Black Panther* was released, so there's a whole group of Wakandans that our fans now love – that was a perfect storm, I believe. Audiences wanted something big to happen, a giant battle. The fight was on. Obviously, the ending was unexpected, but, fortunately, there's another movie to wrap it up.

How satisfying was it for you when you first saw Thanos on screen?

LD: The first time we had seen the potential for it was in a test. [Josh Brolin] came in, and he was just ad-libbing, doing some lines. We sent it out to a VFX company; they rendered the test, and we called [Josh] in to show him. It was remarkable. This was rough, rough stages, but the potential was obviously there.

He is so charismatic as a villain, and he is so resolute in his determination, it is impossible not to like him, even though you're hating him. I think that performance is so formidable. He's the only thing that could battle all of these Super Heroes. [When we] started teasing

01 Teaser poster art for Marvel Studios' *Avengers: Endgame*

02 Thanos as he appears in Marvel Studios' *Avengers: Endgame*

> "How often does the villain win in such a resounding way that you lose approximately half your Super Heroes...?"
> **- Louis D'Esposito**

him in 2012, we were saying to ourselves behind the scenes, "He's got to be good." I mean, six years in the making: he's coming, and he's got to be good. And [Josh] delivered. I'm so proud, getting him to commit to doing this role – and, boy, did he commit.

What do you think it is that Josh Brolin has brought to this role?

TT: As soon as Josh opens up his mouth and his voice comes out, he pretty much is Thanos. It's unbelievable. When he utters all those words... there are so many memorable lines from *Infinity War*, from Thanos' point of view. He's so amazing. He's perfect. You don't want to say that he's such a great bad guy, but he really is an incredible villain. Thanos literally just comes out of him. It's like I said, as soon as he utters the first word, what he brings to the character is so amazing.

Even though Thanos is ostensibly the villain of the piece, audiences do seem to connect with him.

LD: That's what really separates a good villain from a bad: it's somewhat relatable. Maybe if he didn't take such a bad turn he could've been a Super Hero in his own right, but the idea of overpopulation, people starving, his own planet decimated by these things, gave him such a strong reason to go after this goal. He did not want what happened on Titan to happen to the rest of the universe.

At first, he was going from planet to planet. It was analog: "I'll kill off half the people, knowing that this goal will never be achieved at this rate. But if I obtain the six Infinity Stones, the most powerful weapons in the MCU, with the snap of a finger, I could achieve this." Getting the Stones, it was just as fun for me because we'd introduced the Stones in the first *Captain America* film. So, you got to see that fulfillment of obtaining all the Stones, and then Thanos achieving the goal.

Where do we find Thanos just prior to *Endgame*?

TT: We said from the beginning that *Infinity War* is Thanos' movie. We really wanted it to be his film because it's his story. It's about him setting his goal and wanting to accomplish it, wanting to gather all the Stones. He thinks he's doing the right thing, and by doing so, sacrificing half of the universe.

In *Infinity War*, it's Thanos who is really wise, and very smart, and knows what he wants. He was after it, ▶

▶ but along the way he made a lot of sacrifices. His sacrifice of his daughter, Gamora, at the end in Soul World is pretty emotional because she asked him, "What did it cost?" and he said, "Everything." You see that emotion in him; you know that he's lost so much in order to gain this one goal that he's been after all these years, and that really took a toll on him.

So, at the end of the movie you see him walking i   is yurt. He's sitting there, and you see a hint of a smile. But it's a smile that says so much, because he won – he did it, he snapped his fingers – but he also lost his daughter. He lost so much on that journey.

Our heroes are in a completely different state of mind. Each and every one of them are coping with the aftermath of what happened at the end of *Infinity War*.

Where do we find those heroes as *Endgame* opens?
LD: We pick up right where we left off – that's where we thought was the best place. It's so unresolved. You meet our Avengers. They're decimated, obviously broken, sad. But they're still determined.

Robert Downey Jr. was probably the most important casting decision we've ever made. Not only is he a brilliant actor, but he told the world that we are serious about who we hire to play these iconic roles. That allowed for all of the other great actors to come into our universe, knowing that if Robert is doing this, they can do it. So, [Tony Stark] is destined for this. He's been plagued with something happening to our universe since the beginning. He's been foretelling it. He wanted a shield around Earth. No one would listen to him. He's been plagued with nightmares.

Would it be fair to say that the directors of *Infinity War* and *Endgame*, the Russo brothers, have faced quite the challenge with these movies?
LD: The Russo brothers are obviously such accomplished filmmakers, and they've been here before. They know how to handle these things. It's handling the humor, the emotion, and the spectacle all in one, which makes it truly remarkable.

Is that what made them the right directors for these two films?
LD: Kevin and I were discussing who was going to direct these two *Avengers* films, because we came up with this idea, "Let's shoot them together." It seemed like a great idea at the time, but it turned out to be a nightmare, because it's impossible to juggle one story. Could you imagine trying to juggle two stories that are this complicated? It's a case of figuring out what they are, how they intertwine, what comes first and so on...

passionate about what they do. They love this world, and they love the MCU, and all they want to do is build upon that and create more.

03 The heroes unite

Thor has quite the ride in *Infinity War*...
TT: I think Thor had one of the best journeys in *Infinity War*. We start off with him on the ark. He gets defeated by Thanos, and he gets put together with the Guardians for the first time, which is really interesting to see. But he really gets onto this journey in Nidavellir to try to find the weapon, Stormbreaker, the one weapon that can kill Thanos.

At the end, that is one of the best moments ever when he lands with Stormbreaker in Wakanda with Groot and Rocket by his side, ready to kill Thanos. He gets that chance at the end but realizes that it doesn't kill him, because he should've gone for the head based on what Thanos said. It really devastates him. He feels like he's failed his people. He's failed himself, and he's failed to really save the universe when he didn't defeat Thanos when he had the opportunity.

What about Black Widow? What has Natasha brought to these two films and the prior movies?
LD: I think a number of things. There's a mystery about her, because you never can tell exactly what side she's on. I think over the years you've seen she's on the side of what's right, and always making the right decision, but the fun about it is you never know. You can't tell. What is she going to do? What are her real motives? I think the scene in the first *Avengers* with Loki, when she one-ups him, is great. There is also a scene in that movie when she's captured and she escapes. It shows off the abilites that she has, such as her fighting ability, the will, and the strength to keep on going.

Her relationship with Hawkeye is something to explore. Who is her real family? Then in *Civil War*, making the decisions to try to keep that team together and to do what's right. I think it's that combination of her checkered past, her being a super spy, and also her always wanting to do the right thing.

Marvel Studios movies do seem to have kept up with the times in that they have featured strong female characters.
TT: It's very important for us to be able to shine a light on it, because just as many little girls are watching Marvel Studios movies as little boys. To be able to have a group of female heroes for them to look up to, that's something that we definitely need to do. I think Marvel Studios has always been great about listening to the audience and really listening to the public.

I am so glad that *Black Panther* showcased the Dora Milaje in such a cool and awesome way, because they were amazing. They were fighters, and you have Okoye, who's the general – she's tough, she's the badass, and that really is a step further. Then with our first female hero release with *Captain Marvel*, I'm very excited for everybody to see that. ▶

We were going to cross-board them – cross-boarding means we shoot one scene from *Avengers: Infinity War*, one scene from *Endgame*. That slowly disappeared, and we decided to shoot one film at a time – concurrently though – and then trying to figure this out, who should we have helm this ship? Well, I don't think there was any other choice. It had to be the Russo brothers.

The Russos are so adept at handling complicated storylines and dealing with multiple issues. They're great at comedy – that's where they started, that's where their chops are. They've become great at action – they're the premiere action directors – and they're great with emotion. If you look at *Civil War*, for instance – how emotional is that film? So, they were the perfect combination, and we needed two people that were going to be able to shoot for a year straight. That is a remarkable amount of shooting. It would be relentless, because you're constantly prepping, shooting, and editing as you go. There was no other choice.

When we approached them with it, they were wide-eyed and smiling and said, yes, we're up for this task. It was rough on them. There were some illnesses along the way, colds and flus and things like that. But they managed through it.
TT: I've had the privilege to work with them since *The Winter Soldier*, when they first started with us, and I was able to continue along with them on *Civil War*, and now making these two movies. They're perfect for this job. They love these characters, they know these characters inside out. You could not have asked for better directors to be making these two movies, because they're so

"This is the biggest movie that Marvel Studios has ever made. The scope of this film is unheard of." - Trinh Tran

▶ **LD:** We've always had strong women characters in our films. With *Ant-Man and The Wasp* we had the shared title. Agent Carter was our first Super Hero – it was a TV show, but it was our first foray into a female Super Hero. Now *Captain Marvel*, our first solo title. It was always the common belief that maybe having a female as the lead in a Super Hero film would not be financially viable. I think that has been proven undoubtedly 100 per cent wrong.

02

If we can tell interesting stories with women, men, all races, all creeds, all religions, we're going to. Our world is diverse. We need to make films that portray society as it is, and people are going to keep coming to the movies. *Black Panther* was a cultural phenomenon. Basically, 95 per cent an African-American cast, and look how well it does. We are breaking through those barriers. There's no more ceiling above us. We have shattered through it, and we're excited to explore all the Super Heroes from all different backgrounds in the future.

How important are the VFX to this film?
TT: We couldn't do this movie without our visual effects team. They are incredible. We were trying to count off the top of our head how many shots are non-CG, and you can literally count them on one hand. It's incredible how almost every single shot in this movie is pretty much CG. Everything is wrapped around in green screen or blue screen...

What can you tell us about the work of the stunt team on this movie, and in particular Stunt Coordinator Monique Ganderton?
TT: She's amazing. She's doing a great job during our additional photography. I'm so happy to actually see a female department head in that way. But she's offering so much incredible fight choreography to this team. A lot of the fights were completed in principle photography, but we were missing quite a big element in our final battle. So, to be able to have her come in here and just go straight in and start giving us all of these great fights for each and every one of our characters, she's doing an amazing job.

What can you tell us about Production Designer Charles Wood's work on the film?.
TT: To work within our budget, Charlie is so amazing in a way where he's able to rework existing material.

Early on, before Nidavellir came about, we had a whole sequence: we had set the stage for Niflheim. That was a whole different planet with a cave and everything. He actually started building that, and it was in progress. We decided halfway along the way that we were going to change the story and have it be in Nidavellir. Thor is supposed to head over there and meet Eitri. So, the whole set got transformed. But what's so genius about Charlie is that he took that and reworked the material into Nidavellir and completely transformed it. Then he would use some of that existing set and create other environments, because we were being very conscientious about the money that we were spending. So, he's great at that.

What does Costume Designer Judianna Makovsky bring to *Endgame*?
TT: We've been working with Judianna since *The Winter Solider*, and we've kept her on *Civil War* and these last two movies because she's amazing. It is a work of art. She is so meticulous with her designs, paying attention to every single detail that she puts into each and every one of those costumes. She took it upon herself to really take that all in but craft it in a way where it all fits into *Infinity War* and *Endgame*. Her work speaks for itself. She really listens to what we're after, and she takes that into consideration. She works hard at bringing these amazing, beautiful costumes to life.

How does it feel to have finally reached *Endgame*, in every sense of the word?
TT: To be able to start from the beginning and go on the entire journey all the way to the end – I can't even state the feelings that I'm going through. It's extremely exciting. To be able to spend that year and a half in Atlanta with the crew was a great experience. We all love working with each other, but to be able to spend that much time and put in all the work and have everybody embrace it was fantastic.

Everybody was so excited for *Infinity War* when they watched it. It was really sad at the end – everybody came out all shocked – but they were so excited that this was something different, and it was nice to have the different characters come together from the different franchises. But then for this next one, everybody's really anticipating what's going to happen next. What's going to happen with our characters?

I'm so excited for them to see it, but I also don't want the journey to end, because that means we're going to have to shut off the camera, we're going to have to shut down the stages, and it's going to be over in the next couple of days. I don't want it to end. But I'm really excited to get this movie out for everybody to see, because we can't hold on to it any longer.

What will this film deliver for audiences?
LD: I'm sitting on the edge of my seat waiting for this film to come out. I cannot wait to see the reaction. We never have any idea what it will be, especially with this one, because it's so important to us and to our franchise.
TT: It is the biggest movie that Marvel Studios has ever made. The scope of this film is unheard of. When Tony Stark utters the words, "It's been leading to this. It's all been leading to this," it is true. Doctor Strange says it so perfectly at the end of *Infinity War*: "We're now in the endgame." This is it. This is the big, epic showdown of all showdowns. Ⓐ

MARVEL STUDIOS

IRON MAN

MARVEL STUDIOS

IRON MAN 2

MARVEL STUDIOS

THE AVENGERS

MARVEL STUDIOS

ANT-MAN

MARVEL STUDIOS

THOR RAGNAROK

MARVEL STUDIOS

AVENGERS: INFINITY WAR

MARVEL STUDIOS

ANT-MAN AND THE WASP

MARVEL LIBRARY

MARVEL STUDIOS MOVIE SPECIALS

Spider-Man:
Far From Home:
The Official Movie Special

Captain Marvel:
The Official Movie Special

Marvel Studios:
The First Ten Years:
The Official Collector's Edition

Ant-Man and The Wasp:
The Official Movie Special

Avengers: Infinity War:
The Official Movie Special

Black Panther
The Official Movie Companion

Black Panther
The Official Movie Special

Thor: Ragnarok
The Official Movie Special

MARVEL NOVELS

Spider-Man:
Hostile Takeover

Captain Marvel:
Liberation Run

Avengers:
Infinity

Thanos:
Death Sentence

Black Panther:
Who is the
Black Panther?

The Avengers:
Everybody Wants to
Rule the World

Civil War

OTHER TITLES AVAILABLE:

Ant-Man: Natural Enemy
Deadpool: Paws
Spider-Man Forever Young
Venom: Lethal Protector
Spider-Man: Kraven's Last Hunt
(On sale May 28 2019)

DELUXE "ART OF" BOOKS

Marvel's Spider-Man:
The Art of the Game

The Art of Iron Man
(10th Anniversary Edition)

Marvel: Conquest of Champions:
The Art of the Battlerealm